D1327867

£1.29
7/3811

5 Minute Nursery Rhymes

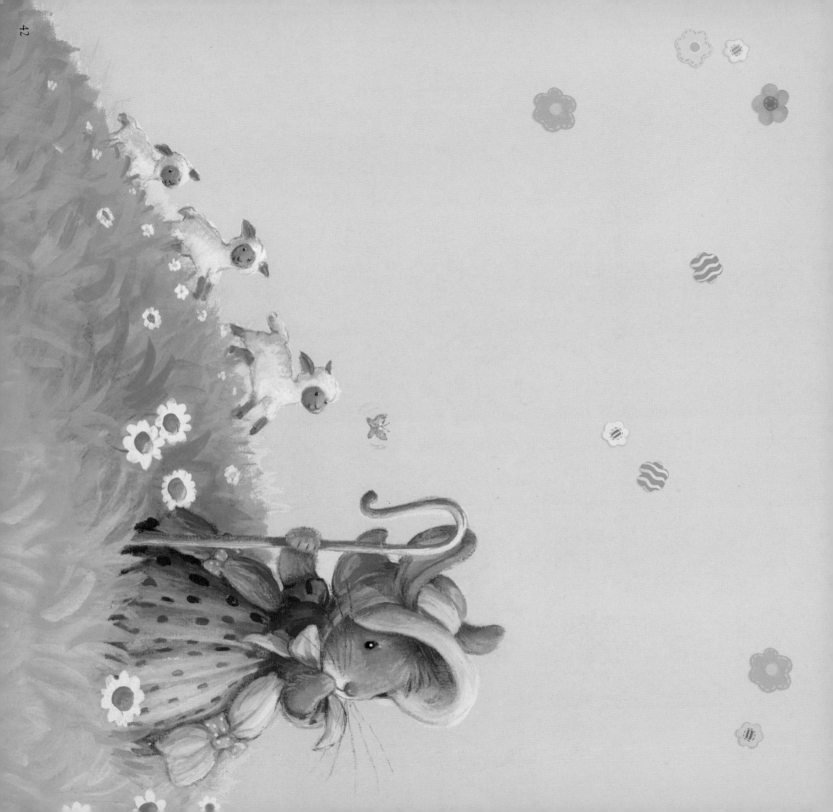

The Grand Old Duke of York

The grand old Duke of York,
He had ten thousand men,
He marched them up to the top of the hill,
And he marched them down again.

And when they were up, they were up,
And when they were down, they were down,
And when they were only halfway up,
They were neither up nor down.

Five Green and Speckled Frogs

Five green and speckled frogs,
Sat on a speckled log,
Eating the most delicious bugs!
One jumped into the pool,
Where it was nice and cool.
Then there were four green and speckled frogs!
Glug! Glug! Glug! Glug!

Four green and speckled frogs,
Sat on a speckled log,
Eating the most delicious bugs!
One jumped into the pool,
Where it was nice and cool.
Then there were three green and speckled frogs!
Glug! Glug! Glug!

Three green and speckled frogs,
Sat on a speckled log,
Eating the most delicious bugs!
One jumped into the pool,
Where it was nice and cool.
Then there were two green and speckled frogs!
Glug! Glug!

Two green and speckled frogs,
Sat on a speckled log,
Eating the most delicious bugs!
One jumped into the pool,
Where it was nice and cool.
Then there was one green and speckled frog!
Glug!

One green and speckled frog,
Sat on a speckled log,
Eating the most delicious bugs!
He jumped into the pool,
Where it was nice and cool.
Then there were no green and speckled frogs!

Three Blind Mice

Three blind mice, three blind mice,
See how they run! See how they run!
They all ran after the farmer's wife,
Who cut off their tails with a carving knife.
Did ever you see such a thing in your life
As three blind mice?

Here is the Beehive

Here is the beehive. Where are the bees?
Hidden away where nobody sees.

Watch and you'll see them
come out of the hive,
one, two, three, four, five.

Bzzzzzzz!

Over in the Meadow

Over in the meadow,
In the sand in the sun,
Lived an old mother froggy,
And her little froggy one.
"Wink!" said the mother.
"I wink!" said the one.
So they winked and they blinked,
In the sand in the sun.

Over in the meadow,
Where the stream runs blue,
Lived an old mother fish,
And her little fishes two.
"Swim!" said the mother.
"We swim!" said the two.
So they swam and they leaped,
Where the stream runs blue.

Over in the meadow,
In a hole in a tree,
Lived an old mother bluebird,
And her little birdies three.
"Sing!" said the mother.
"We sing!" said the three.
So they sang and were glad,
In the hole in the tree.

37

One, Two,
Stars on High

One, two – stars on high,
Three, four – in the sky.
Five, six – burning bright,
Seven, eight – in the night.
Nine, ten – I declare,
Too many stars to count up there!

Five in the Bed

There were five in the bed
And the little one said,
"Roll over, roll over!"
So they all rolled over,
And one fell out . . .

There were four in the bed
And the little one said,
"Roll over, roll over!"
So they all rolled over,
And one fell out . . .

There were three in the bed
And the little one said,
"Roll over, roll over!"
So they all rolled over,
And one fell out . . .

There were two in the bed
And the little one said,
"Roll over, roll over!"
So they all rolled over,
And one fell out . . .

There was one in the bed,
And the little one said,
"Goodnight!"

Incy Wincy Spider,
can you see him now?
He's fluttered onto Buttercup,
the black and white young cow.

MOOOO! says Buttercup
and flicks her long, wide ears.
And Incy Wincy Spider
spins off and disappears!

MOOOO!

Little Bo-Peep's Favourite Farmyard Rhymes

Baa, Baa, Black Sheep

"Baa, baa, black sheep, have you any wool?"

"Yes sir, yes sir, three bags full.

One for the master, and one for the dame,

And one for the little boy who lives down the lane."

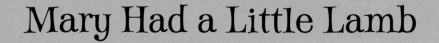

Mary Had a Little Lamb

Mary had a little lamb,
Its fleece was white as snow,
And everywhere that Mary went,
The lamb was sure to go.

Little Bo-Peep

Little Bo-Peep has lost her sheep,
And doesn't know where to find them.
Leave them alone, and they'll come home,
Bringing their tails behind them.

Six Little Ducks

Six little ducks that I once knew,
Fat ducks, pretty ducks they were too,
But the one little duck with the feather on his back,
He led the others with his *Quack! Quack! Quack!*

Down to the meadow they would go,
Wig-wag, wiggle-wag, to and fro,
But the one little duck with the feather on his back,
He led the others with his *Quack! Quack! Quack!*

Cock-a-doodle-doo!

Cock-a-doodle-doo!
My dame has lost her shoe.
My master's lost his fiddlestick,
And knows not what to do.

Old MacDonald Had a Farm

Old MacDonald had a farm,
E-I-E-I-O!
And on that farm he had some sheep,
E-I-E-I-O!

Sleep, Baby, Sleep

Sleep, baby, sleep.
Your father guards the sheep.
Your mother shakes the dreamland tree,
Down falls a little dream for thee.
Sleep, baby, sleep.

Jack and Jill's Favourite Playtime Rhymes

Jack Be Nimble

Jack be nimble,
Jack be quick.
Jack jump over
The candlestick.

Ring-a-ring o' Roses

Ring-a-ring o' roses,
A pocket full of posies,
A-tishoo! A-tishoo!
We all fall down.

B-I-N-G-O

There was a farmer who had a dog,
And Bingo was his name-o.
B-I-N-G-O
B-I-N-G-O
B-I-N-G-O
And Bingo was his name-o.

There was a farmer who had a dog,
And Bingo was his name-o.
(clap)-I-N-G-O
(clap)-I-N-G-O
(clap)-I-N-G-O
And Bingo was his name-o.

There was a farmer who had a dog,
And Bingo was his name-o.
(clap)-(clap)-N-G-O
(clap)-(clap)-N-G-O
(clap)-(clap)-N-G-O
And Bingo was his name-o.

There was a farmer who had a dog,
And Bingo was his name-o.
(clap)-(clap)-(clap)-G-O
(clap)-(clap)-(clap)-G-O
(clap)-(clap)-(clap)-G-O
And Bingo was his name-o.

There was a farmer who had a dog,
And Bingo was his name-o.
(clap)-(clap)-(clap)-(clap)-O
(clap)-(clap)-(clap)-(clap)-O
(clap)-(clap)-(clap)-(clap)-O
And Bingo was his name-o.

There was a farmer who had a dog,
And Bingo was his name-o.
(clap)-(clap)-(clap)-(clap)-(clap)
(clap)-(clap)-(clap)-(clap)-(clap)
(clap)-(clap)-(clap)-(clap)-(clap)
And Bingo was his name-o.

Row, Row, Row Your Boat

Row, row, row your boat,
Gently down the stream.
Merrily, merrily, merrily, merrily,
Life is but a dream!

The Wheels on the Bus

The wheels on the bus go
ROUND and ROUND,
ROUND and ROUND,
ROUND and ROUND . . .

The wheels on the bus go
ROUND and ROUND,
All day long!

The wipers on the bus go
SWISH! SWISH! SWISH!
SWISH! SWISH! SWISH!
SWISH! SWISH! SWISH! . . .

. . . The wipers on the bus go
SWISH! SWISH! SWISH!
All day long!

The bags on the bus go
BUMP! BUMP! BUMP!
BUMP! BUMP! BUMP!
BUMP! BUMP! BUMP! . . .

. . . The bags on the bus go
BUMP! BUMP! BUMP!
All day long!

95

The bell on the bus goes
DING! DING! DING!
DING! DING! DING!
DING! DING! DING! . . .

. . . The bell on the bus goes
DING! DING! DING!
All day long!

The brakes on the bus go
SQUEAK! SQUEAK! SQUEAK!
SQUEAK! SQUEAK! SQUEAK!
SQUEAK! SQUEAK! SQUEAK! . . .

... The brakes on the bus go
SQUEAK! SQUEAK! SQUEAK!
All day long!

The horn on the bus goes
TOOT! TOOT! TOOT!
TOOT! TOOT! TOOT!
TOOT! TOOT! TOOT! . . .

The horn on the bus goes
TOOT! TOOT! TOOT!
All day long!

105

Skip to My Lou

Skip, skip, skip to my Lou,
Skip, skip, skip to my Lou,
Skip, skip, skip to my Lou,
Skip to my Lou, my darling!

Lost my partner, what will I do?
Lost my partner, what will I do?
Lost my partner, what will I do?
Skip to my Lou, my darling!

I'll get another one just like you!
I'll get another one just like you!
I'll get another one just like you!
Skip to my Lou, my darling!

Skip, skip, skip to my Lou,
Skip, skip, skip to my Lou,
Skip, skip, skip to my Lou,
Skip to my Lou, my darling!

Jack and Jill

Jack and Jill went up the hill,
To fetch a pail of water.
Jack fell down
And broke his crown,
And Jill came tumbling after.

London Bridge

London Bridge is falling down,
Falling down, falling down.
London Bridge is falling down,
My fair lady!

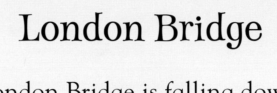

If You're Happy and You Know It

If you're happy and you know it,
clap your hands.
If you're happy and you know it,
clap your hands.
If you're happy and you know it,
And you really want to show it,
If you're happy and you know it,
clap your hands.

If you're happy and you know it,
stomp your feet.
If you're happy and you know it,
stomp your feet.
If you're happy and you know it,
And you really want to show it,
If you're happy and you know it,
stomp your feet.

If you're happy and you know it,
shout, "Hooray!"
If you're happy and you know it,
shout, "Hooray!"
If you're happy and you know it,
And you really want to show it,
If you're happy and you know it,
shout, "Hooray!"

See-saw,
Margery Daw

See-saw, Margery Daw,
Johnny shall have a new master.
He shall have but a penny a day,
Because he can't work any faster.

Head, Shoulders, Knees and Toes

Head, shoulders, knees and toes,
Head, shoulders, knees and toes,
Eyes and ears and mouth and nose,
Head, shoulders, knees and toes!

Teddy Bear,
Teddy Bear

Teddy bear, teddy bear,
Touch your nose.

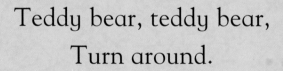

Teddy bear, teddy bear,
Touch your toes.

Teddy bear, teddy bear,
Turn around.

Teddy bear, teddy bear,
Touch the ground.

Teddy bear, teddy bear,
Go upstairs.

Teddy bear, teddy bear,
Say your prayers.

Teddy bear, teddy bear,
Turn out the light.

Teddy bear, teddy bear,
Say goodnight.

115

Incy Wincy Spider's Favourite Animal Rhymes

Little Miss Muffet

Little Miss Muffet
Sat on a tuffet,
Eating her curds and whey.

Along came a spider,
Who sat down beside her,
And frightened
Miss Muffet away.

Ladybird, Ladybird

Ladybird, ladybird, fly away home,
Your house is on fire, and your children are gone,
All except one, and that's little Ann,
For she crept under the frying pan.

Incy Wincy Spider

Incy Wincy Spider
Climbed up the water spout.
Down came the rain
And washed poor Incy out.
Out came the sunshine
And dried up all the rain.
And Incy Wincy Spider
Climbed up the spout again.

Incy Wincy
Goes Flying

Whooo!

Incy Wincy Spider,
playing on a farm,
Spinning silver silk webs
high up in a barn.

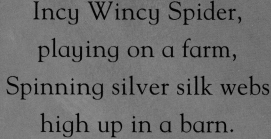

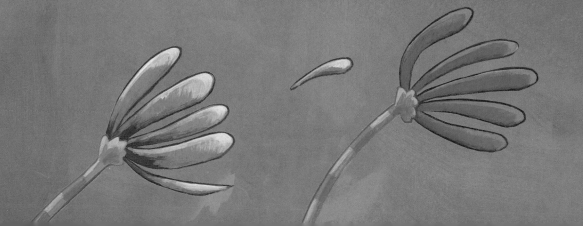

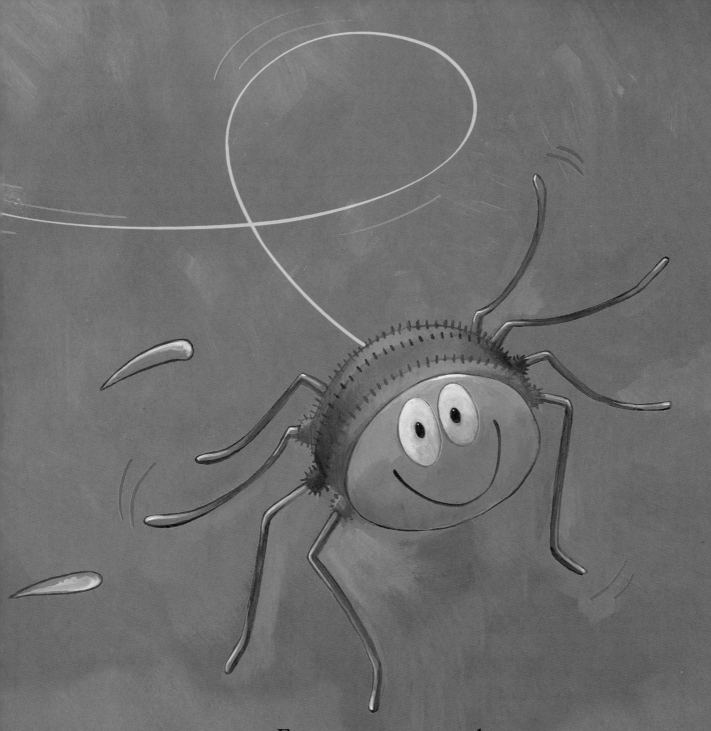

From an open window,
a gust of wind blows WHOOO!

whooooosh

And Incy Wincy Spider
with a WHOOOOOSH goes too!

Incy Wincy Spider
is flying, there he goes!
He drifts onto a pink pig
and dangles from its nose.

OINKKK! grunts the pig
with Incy climbing up his snout.
And Incy Wincy Spider
is catapulted out!

Incy Wincy Spider,
he doesn't think it funny.
He's tangled on a grey goat
and calls out for his mummy.

B-E-H-H-H! bleats the goat,
who shakes from side to side.
And Incy Wincy Spider
begins another ride!

Behhhh!

Incy Wincy Spider,
gliding through the air.
He hangs onto a duck's beak
and tickles under there.

QUACK! honks the yellow duck
and gives a great big sneeze.
And Incy Wincy Spider
floats off in the breeze!

Incy Wincy Spider,
what a dizzy day!
He's settled on a brown horse
chewing clumps of hay.

Nei

NEIGHHHH! snorts the horse
and jumps up really high.
And Incy Wincy Spider
pings off through the sky!

ghhhh!

Incy Wincy Spider
zooms past something red.
He shoots out lines of web silk
and sticks to cockerel's head.

COCK-A-DOODLE-DOO!

The red and green
cockerel crows
COCK-A-DOODLE-DOO!
But Incy Wincy Spider,
where on earth are you?

138

Incy Wincy Spider,
what's he stuck on now?
A goat, horse or cockerel?
A pig, duck or cow?

No, he bounces with a

BOINNGGG!

Hooray! It's Mummy's web!
Now Incy Wincy Spider
is safely home in bed!

Pussy Cat, Pussy Cat

"Pussy cat, pussy cat,
Where have you been?"
"I've been to London
To visit the Queen."

"Pussy cat, pussy cat,
What did you there?"
"I frightened a little mouse
Under the chair."

The Owl and the Pussy Cat

The owl and the pussy cat went to sea
In a beautiful pea-green boat.
They took some honey
and plenty of money,
Wrapped up in a five-pound note.

The owl looked up to the stars above,
And sang to a small guitar,
"O, lovely Pussy! O, Pussy, my love,
What a beautiful Pussy you are, you are, you are,
What a beautiful Pussy you are!"

Come to the Window

Come to the window,
My baby, with me,
And look at the stars
That shine on the sea.

144

There are two little stars
That play bo-peep.
And two little fish
Far down in the deep.
And two little frogs
Cry, "Neap, neap, neap.
I see a dear baby
That should be asleep!"

145

Where Has My Little Dog Gone?

Oh where, oh where has my little dog gone?

Oh where, oh where can he be?

With his ears cut short and his tail cut long,

Oh where, oh where can he be?

All the Pretty Little Horses

Hush-a-bye, don't you cry,
Go to sleep, my little baby.

When you wake you will have
All the pretty little horses.
Blacks and greys, dapples and bays,
Coach and six little horses.

Hush, Little Baby

Hush, little baby, don't say a word,
Papa's gonna buy you a mockingbird.
And if that mockingbird don't sing,
Papa's gonna buy you a diamond ring.
And if that diamond ring turns to brass,
Papa's gonna buy you a looking glass.
And if that looking glass gets broke,
Papa's gonna buy you a billy goat.

And if that billy goat don't pull,
Papa's gonna buy you a cart and bull.
And if that cart and bull turn over,
Papa's gonna buy you a dog named Rover.
And if that dog named Rover don't bark,
Papa's gonna buy you a horse and cart.
And if that horse and cart fall down,
You'll still be the sweetest little baby in town.

Little Jack Horner's Favourite Food Rhymes

Pat-a-cake

Pat-a-cake, pat-a-cake,
Baker's man!
Bake me a cake
As fast as you can.
Pat it and prick it
And mark it with 'B',
And put it in the oven
For Baby and me.

Hot Cross Buns

Hot cross buns!

Hot cross buns!

One ha' penny, two ha' penny,

Hot cross buns!

This Little Piggy

This little piggy went to market.

This little piggy stayed at home.

This little piggy had roast beef.

This little piggy had none.

And this little piggy cried,
"Wee wee wee!" all the way home.

Peter, Peter, Pumpkin Eater

Peter, Peter, pumpkin eater,
Had a wife and couldn't keep her.
He put her in a pumpkin shell,
And there he kept her very well.

Little Jack Horner

Little Jack Horner
Sat in the corner,
Eating a Christmas pie.
He put in his thumb,
And pulled out a plum,
And said,
"What a good boy am I!"

Old King Cole

Old King Cole
Was a merry old soul,
And a merry old soul was he.
He called for his pipe,
And he called for his bowl,
And he called for his fiddlers three.

Sing a Song of Sixpence

Sing a song of sixpence,
A pocket full of rye.
Four and twenty blackbirds
Baked in a pie.
When the pie was opened,
The birds began to sing.
Wasn't that a dainty dish
To set before the king?

Pease Porridge Hot

Pease porridge hot,
Pease porridge cold.
Pease porridge in the pot,
Nine days old.

Some like it hot,
Some like it cold.
Some like it in the pot,
Nine days old.

The Princess and the Pea

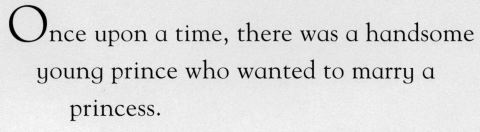

Once upon a time, there was a handsome young prince who wanted to marry a princess.

But she had to be a *real* princess. The prince travelled the world in search of a bride, but none of the princesses he met were quite right. Some were not graceful enough, some didn't know how to curtsy, and some of them didn't smile. Not one of them was a real princess.

So, feeling very disappointed, the prince returned home without a wife.

One night, a terrible storm fell across the kingdom. Lightning flashed, thunder crashed, and the rain poured down.

Suddenly, there came a knock at the palace gate.

When the king went to see who it was, he couldn't believe his eyes! There stood a princess. But she was in a terrible state! Rain dripped from her nose right down to the tips of her toes.

"May I come in?" asked the princess. "I got lost in the storm and now I'm soaking wet."

The king invited her in, and when the prince saw her, he thought she was the most beautiful princess he'd ever seen!

But the queen wasn't so sure that
she was a real princess.

"We shall soon find out," said
the queen, as she called her maids
to prepare a bed for the princess.
Upon the bed they placed a tiny
green pea, and they piled twenty
mattresses on top of it.

"Only a real princess," said
the queen, "could have skin
that is delicate enough to feel
that tiny pea."

The princess climbed to the top of the
very tall bed, and there she was to sleep all night.

The following morning, the queen asked the princess how she had slept.

"Terribly!" replied the princess. "There was something hard in the bed which made me toss and turn all night."

"*You're a real princess!*" cried the prince, and the king and queen smiled with delight.

The prince and princess fell in love, and the king and queen arranged a grand wedding, inviting everyone in the kingdom . . .

And they all lived happily ever after!

So if you ever feel a small lump in your bed, maybe you're a real princess too!

Sippity Sup

Sippity sup, sippity sup,
Bread and milk from a china cup.
Bread and milk from a bright silver spoon,
Made of a piece of the bright silver moon.

The Muffin Man

Do you know the muffin man,
The muffin man, the muffin man?
Do you know the muffin man,
Who lives in Drury Lane?

Oats, Peas, Beans and Barley

Oats, peas, beans and barley grow,
Oats, peas, beans and barley grow.
Can you or I or anyone know
How oats, peas, beans and barley grow?

First the farmer sows his seed,
Stands up tall and takes his ease.
He stamps his foot and claps his hands,
And turns around to view his lands.

To Market, To Market

To market, to market, to buy a fat pig.
Home again, home again, jiggety-jig.
To market, to market, to buy a fat hog.
Home again, home again, jiggety-jog.

Hey Diddle Diddle

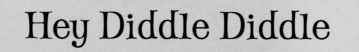

Hey diddle diddle,
The cat and the fiddle,
The cow jumped over the moon.

The little dog laughed, to see such fun,
And the dish ran away with the spoon.

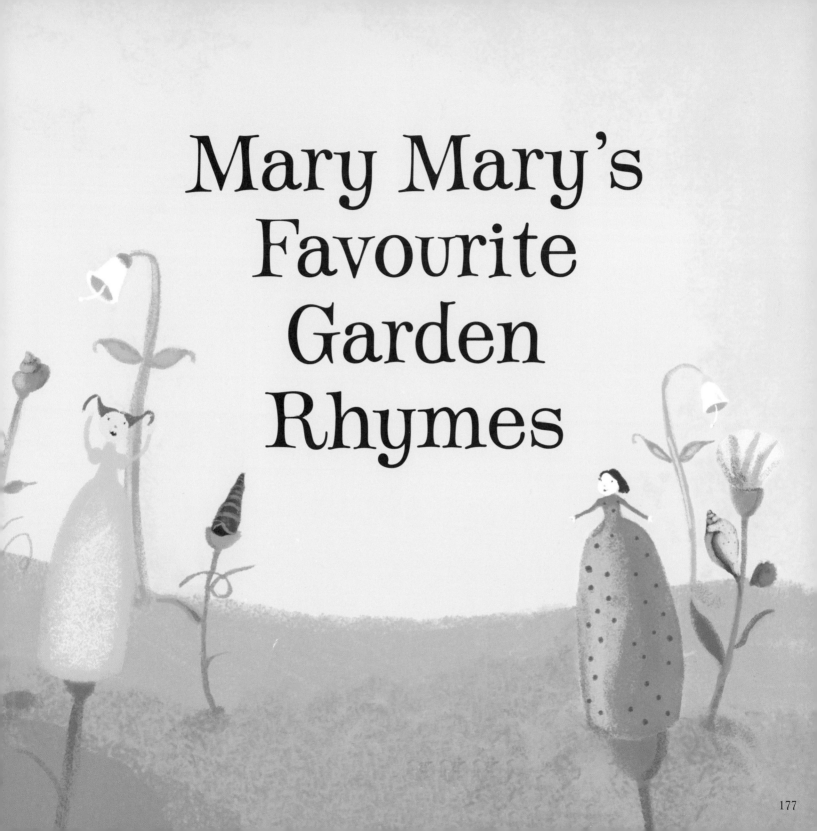

Mary Mary's Favourite Garden Rhymes

Here We Go Round the Mulberry Bush

Here we go round the mulberry bush,
The mulberry bush,
The mulberry bush.
Here we go round the mulberry bush,
So early in the morning.

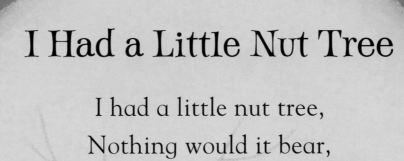

I Had a Little Nut Tree

I had a little nut tree,
Nothing would it bear,
But a silver nutmeg
And a golden pear.
The King of Spain's daughter
Came to visit me,
And all for the sake of
My little nut tree.

Mary Mary, Quite Contrary

"Mary Mary, quite contrary,
How does your garden grow?"

"With silver bells,
And cockle shells,
And pretty maids
All in a row."

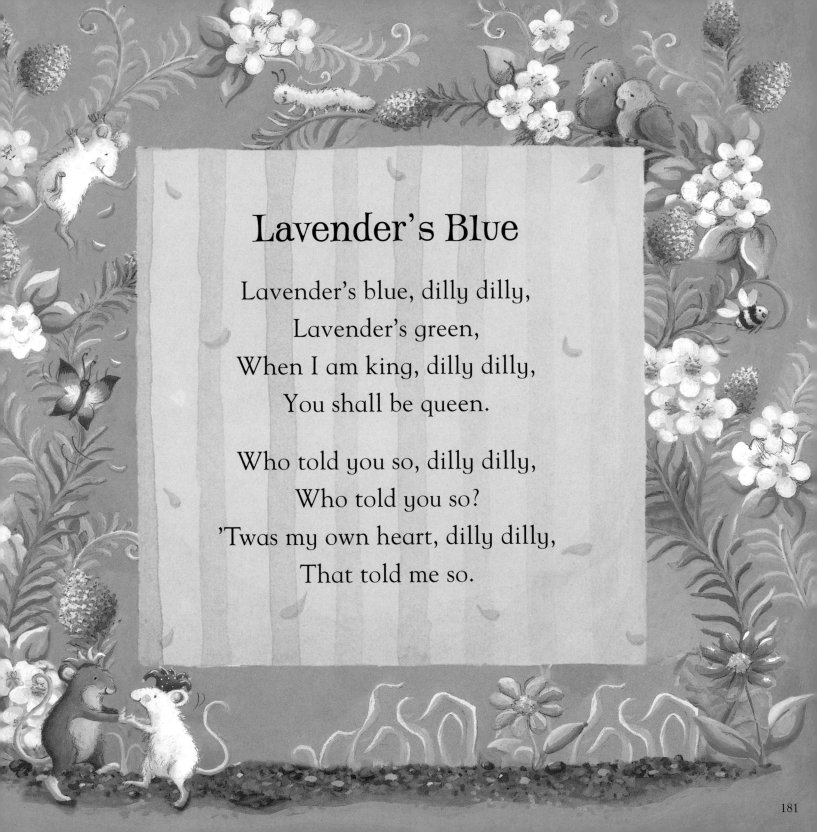

Lavender's Blue

Lavender's blue, dilly dilly,
Lavender's green,
When I am king, dilly dilly,
You shall be queen.

Who told you so, dilly dilly,
Who told you so?
'Twas my own heart, dilly dilly,
That told me so.

Roses are Red

Roses are red,
Violets are blue.
Sugar is sweet,
And so are you!

One Magical Morning

In the shadowy woods,
one clear summer's morning,
Mummy took Little Bear
to see the day dawning.

The bears walked together
through grass drenched with dew.
Little Bear skipped,
as little bears do.

As the silvery moon
faded high in the sky,
Twinkle-eyed voles
came scurrying by.

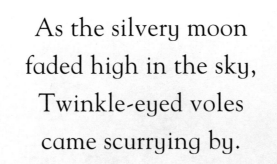

And a little mouse gazed
as the morning sun
Melted the stars away,
one by one.

Fox cubs played while
the mist swirled like smoke,
Wrapping the trees
in its wispy cloak.

A pigeon coo-cooed
from a branch way up high.
Little Bear laughed,
"Look at me! Watch me fly!"

They stopped for a drink
at a babbling stream,
And the sun turned the forest
soft pink, gold and green.

"Look, Mummy!" cried
Little Bear in delight.
As a mole burst, blinking,
into the light.

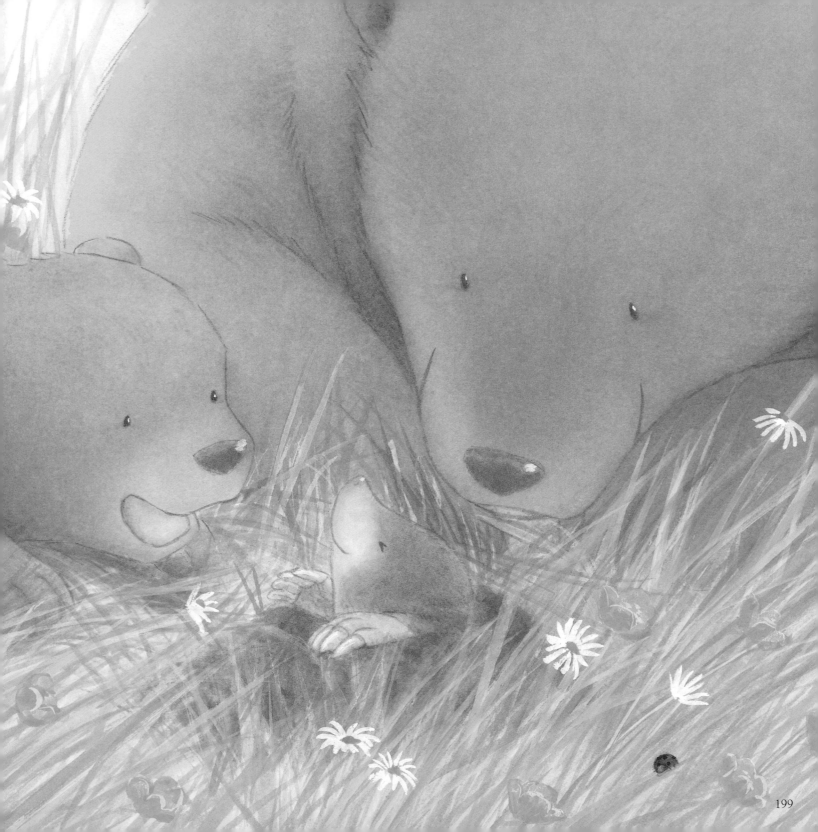

Mummy Bear smiled,
"Over here, take a peep!"
Bear's friend, Little Rabbit,
lay curled up asleep.

"Wake up, Little Rabbit,
come and play in the sun.
It's a beautiful day –
and it's just begun!"

It's Raining, It's Pouring

It's raining, it's pouring,
The old man is snoring.
He went to bed
And bumped his head,
And couldn't get up
in the morning.

Rain, Rain, Go Away

Rain, rain, go away,
Come again another day!

The Green Grass Grew All Around

There once was a tree,
A pretty little tree,
The prettiest little tree
That you ever did see.

Oh, the tree in a hole,
And the hole in the ground,
And the green grass grew all around, all around,
And the green grass grew all around.

Now on this tree
There was a branch,
The prettiest little branch
That you ever did see.

Oh, the branch on the tree,
And the tree in a hole,
And the hole in the ground,
And the green grass grew all around, all around,
And the green grass grew all around.

Now on this branch
There was a bird,
The prettiest little bird
That you ever did see.

Oh, the bird on the branch,
And the branch on the tree,
And the tree in a hole,
And the hole in the ground,
And the green grass grew all around, all around,
And the green grass grew all around.

Early to Bed

Early to bed,
Early to rise,
Makes a man healthy,
wealthy and wise.

Red Sky at Night

Red sky at night,
Shepherd's delight.
Red sky in the morning,
Shepherd's warning.

Brahms' Lullaby

Lullaby and goodnight,
With roses bedight,
With lilies o'er spread,
Is baby's wee bed.
Lay thee down now and rest,
May thy slumber be blessed.
Lay thee down now and rest,
May thy slumber be blessed.

I See the Moon

I see the moon and the moon sees me
Under the shade of the old oak tree.
Please let the light that shines on me
Shine on the one I love.

Little Boy Blue's Favourite Childhood Rhymes

Monday's Child

Monday's child is fair of face,
Tuesday's child is full of grace,
Wednesday's child is full of woe,
Thursday's child has far to go,
Friday's child is loving and giving,
Saturday's child works hard for a living,
But the child that's born
on the Sabbath Day,
Is bonnie, blithe,
good and gay.

Diddle Diddle Dumpling

Diddle diddle dumpling, my son John,
Went to bed with his trousers on.
One shoe off and one shoe on,
Diddle diddle dumpling,
my son John.

There Was a Little Girl

There was a little girl who had a little curl
Right in the middle of her forehead.
When she was good, she was very, very good,
And when she was bad, she was horrid.

Are You Sleeping?

Are you sleeping,
Are you sleeping?
Brother John,
Brother John?
Morning bells are ringing,
Morning bells are ringing,
Ding, ding, dong,
Ding, ding, dong.

Lucy Locket

Lucy Locket lost her pocket,
Kitty Fisher found it.
Not a penny was there in it,
Only ribbon round it.

Little Boy Blue

Little Boy Blue,
Come blow your horn.
The sheep's in the meadow,
The cow's in the corn.
Where is the boy
Who looks after the sheep?
He's under the haystack
Fast asleep.

Lazy Mary

"Lazy Mary, will you get up,
Will you get up, will you get up?
Lazy Mary, will you get up,
Will you get up in the morning?"

"No, dear mother, I won't get up,
I won't get up, I won't get up.
No, no, mother, I won't get up,
I won't get up in the morning."

Goldilocks and the Three Bears

In a fairytale wood lived a bear family.

Mummy and Daddy and Baby made three.

Early one day, they all sat down to eat.

The table was laid and the breakfast complete.

With toast in the toaster and tea in the pot,

And on the stove, porridge was steaming and hot.

"My porridge is boiling," said Dad with a frown.

"Let's walk in the wood and let it cool down."

But just as they left and strolled out in the sun,
Along came young Goldilocks, looking for fun.
She rang on the doorbell, but no one replied,
Then bold as can be, she walked straight inside!
She crept to the kitchen with a rumbling tummy,
Saw three bowls of porridge and whispered, "Oh yummy!"

One large bowl, one medium, and one small and blue.
She grumbled, "Oh no," when she tried the first two.
"Too hot then too salty – but this one looks good."
She gobbled the lot as fast as she could.

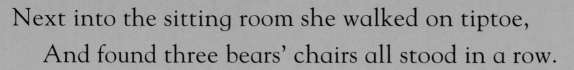

Next into the sitting room she walked on tiptoe,
And found three bears' chairs all stood in a row.
The first chair was Dad's – it was big, tall and strong.
Mum's pink-cushioned chair was the next one along.
Goldilocks sighed, "Oh, they're both much too high.
But I'll give this third little chair a quick try!"

It was Baby Bear's chair and it looked the right size,
So she plonked down her bottom, but got a surprise!
SNAP! CRASH! and CRUMBLE! She fell on the ground,
And pieces of chair were strewn all around.
Cheeky Goldilocks laughed at the mess on the floor.
Still giggling, she sneaked from the room to explore!

In the bears' bedroom, she decided to rest.

But which of the three lovely beds would be best?

"I don't like the big bed – it's hard and cold too.

The second's too soft, but the small one will do!"

Then as Goldilocks slept, as quiet as a mouse,

The three bears came walking back into the house!

"My porridge has gone!" cried poor Baby Bear.
"And who would have broken my favourite chair?"
Goldy opened her eyes and she quivered with fear,
When she saw the three growling bears standing near.
She fled from the house and ran down the lane.
And the three angry bears never saw her again!

Girls and Boys, Come Out to Play

Girls and boys,
come out to play,
The moon does shine
as bright as day.
Leave your supper
and leave your sleep,
And join your playfellows
in the street.

232

Bonnie Girls and Bonnie Boys

Bonnie girls and bonnie boys,
Picking up their bonnie toys.
No more play, it's time for bed,
Time to rest their bonnie heads!

Matthew, Mark, Luke and John

Matthew, Mark, Luke and John,

Bless the bed that I lie on.

Four corners to my bed,

Four angels round my head.

One to watch and one to pray,

And two to guide me through the day.

You're My Little Star

You're my special little star,
I love you night
and day.

I love the sparkle in your smile, and the funny things you say.

When we play roly-poly,
and tumble paws to toes,
I love to hold you tight,
and pop a kiss upon your nose!

You're my little star
when you sing
your songs to me,

And when
we're reading stories,
cuddled cosy as can be.

The stars so bright
light up our night,
how wonderful they are!
But you shine brightest
of them all – you are my
little star!

239

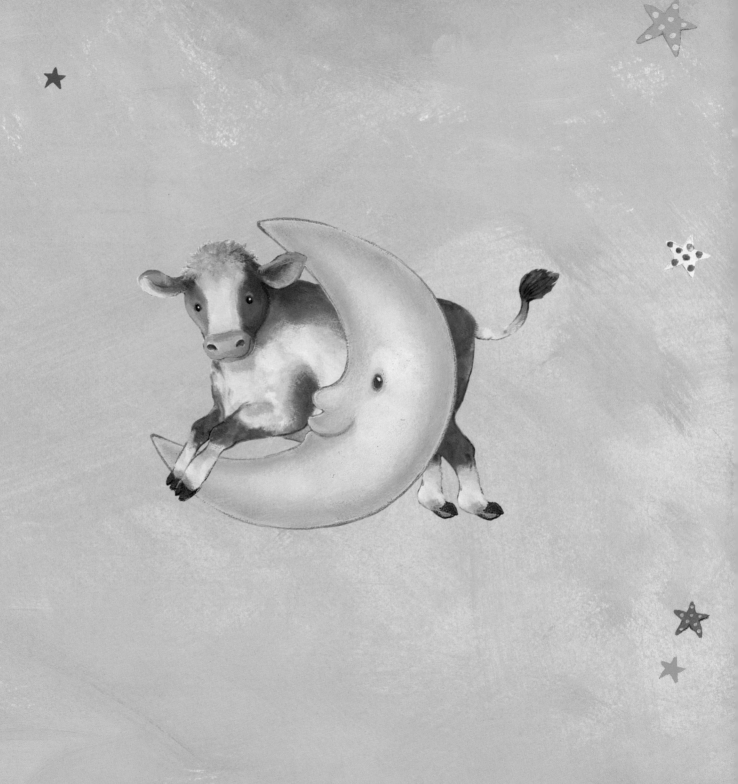

Wee Willie Winkie's Favourite Bedtime Rhymes

Rock-a-bye, Baby

Rock-a-bye, baby, on the tree-top,
When the wind blows, the cradle will rock.
When the bough breaks, the cradle will fall,
And down will come baby, cradle and all.

Star Light, Star Bright

Star light, star bright,
First star I see tonight.
I wish I may, I wish I might,
Have the wish I wish tonight.

Wee Willie Winkie

Wee Willie Winkie
runs through the town,
Upstairs and downstairs,
in his nightgown,
Rapping at the window, crying through the lock,
"Are the children all in bed, for now it's eight o'clock?"

Aiken Drum

There was a man lived in the moon,
In the moon, in the moon,
There was a man lived in the moon,
And his name was Aiken Drum.

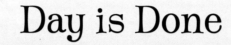

Day is Done

Day is done,
Gone the sun,
From the lake, from the hills,
from the sky.
All is well, safely rest,
God is nigh.

Now the Day is Over

Now the day is over,
Night is drawing nigh,
Shadows of the evening,
Steal across the sky.
Now the darkness gathers,
Stars begin to peep.
Birds and beasts and flowers
Soon will be asleep.

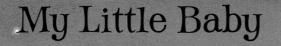

My Little Baby

While you sleep,
The world spins around,
Slowly to rock you,
Safe and sound.
The morning will come.
A new day will break.
And my little baby
From dreams will awake.

A Kiss
Goodnight

Tickle my toes and cuddle me tight,
Just one more game, and then it's goodnight!

Snuggly, huggly, small sleepyhead.
Time to carry you upstairs to bed!

Hush-a-bye, lullaby, sing you to sleep,

Drift on the music that plays soft and deep.

258

Warm in the glow of the lantern's soft beams,
Snuggled together, we're dreaming sweet dreams!

Golden Slumbers

Golden slumbers kiss your eyes,
Smiles await you when you rise.
Sleep, pretty darling, do not cry,
And I will sing a lullaby.

Hush-a-bye, Baby

Hush-a-bye, baby,
Sleep, angel, sleep,
Warm and dry your cradle keep.
When you wake, my little one,
A new day will have just begun.

261

God Bless the Moon

I see the moon,
And the moon sees me.
God bless the moon,
And God bless me.

When the Sun Goes Down to Bed

When the sun goes down to bed,
The stars come out to play.
They dance across the sky all night,
Until the break of day.

All Through the Night

Sleep, my child, and peace attend thee,
All through the night.
Guardian angels God will send thee,
All through the night.

Soft the drowsy hours are creeping,
Hill and vale in slumber steeping,
I my loving vigil keeping,
All through the night.

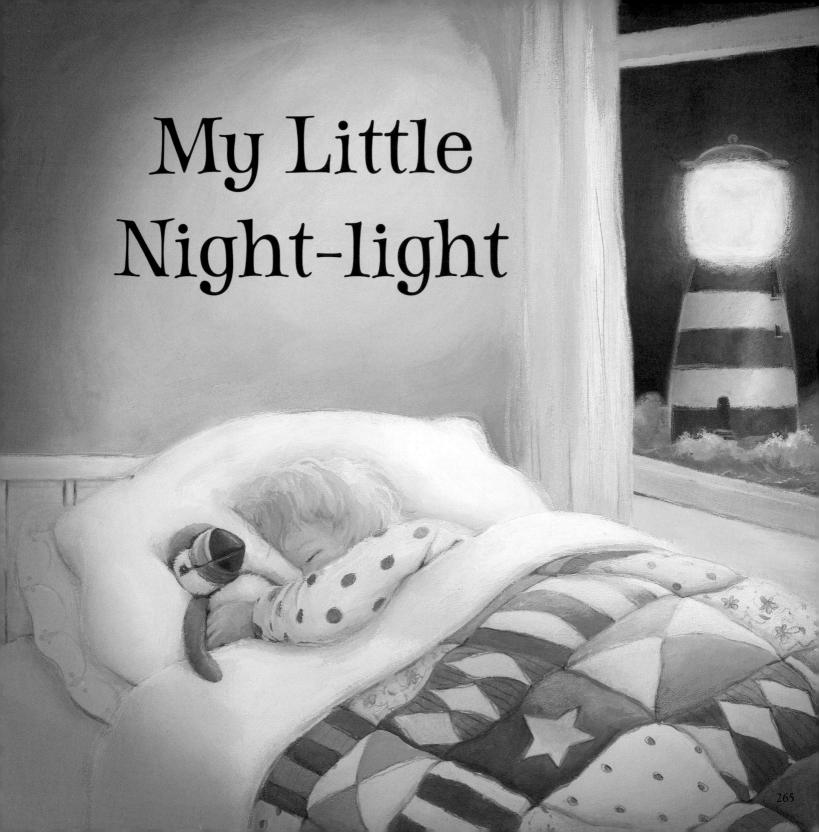

My Little Night-light

The lighthouse by the harbour side
　　Shines brightly through the year.
Like a night-light, always there,
　　Its light beams strong and clear.

Night is falling, bright stars gleam,
　　Little lighthouse, shine your beam.

As darkness comes and shadows creep,
The lighthouse lights the bay.
The dolphins swim towards the glow –
They've one last game to play.

Through the starry, moonlit night,
Little lighthouse, shine your light.

In summertime, as evening falls,
The puffin chicks are fed.
Watched over by the lighthouse beam,
They'll soon be tucked in bed!

Lighthouse, shining all around,
Keep the puffins safe and sound.

271

On stormy nights, when boats get lost,
    And fight through waves and foam,
The lighthouse shines its golden beam
    To lead them safely home.

Little lighthouse, brave and bright,
    Shine on through the darkest night.

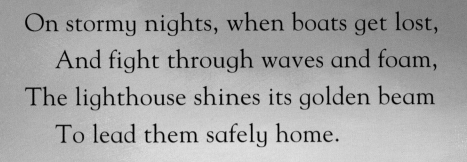

Down by the rock pools, on warm nights,
The crabs come out to play,
And as they scuttle on the sand,
The lighthouse lights their way.

Lighthouse, cast your glowing light –
Turn the rock pools silver-white.

A whale and baby pass the shore,
   The lighthouse beam shines clear.
It lightens up the craggy rocks,
   So they won't swim too near.

Lighthouse, shining round the bay,
   Turn the waves to silver spray.

The mouse takes the cheese, the mouse takes the cheese,
Hi-ho, the derry-o, the mouse takes the cheese.

The cheese stands alone, the cheese stands alone,
Hi-ho, the derry-o, the cheese stands alone.

Hickety Pickety, My Black Hen

Hickety Pickety, my black hen,
She lays eggs for gentlemen.
Sometimes nine and sometimes ten,
Hickety Pickety, my black hen.

Old MacDonald had a farm,
E-I-E-I-O!
And on that farm he had some ducks,
E-I-E-I-O!
With a QUACK! QUACK! here,
And a QUACK! QUACK! there . . .

. . . Here a QUACK!
There a QUACK!
Everywhere a QUACK! QUACK!
Old MacDonald had a farm,
E-I-E-I-O!

Old MacDonald had a farm,
E-I-E-I-O!
And on that farm he had a dog,
E-I-E-I-O!
With a *WOOF! WOOF!* here,
And a *WOOF! WOOF!* there . . .

Woof!
Woof!

. . . Here a WOOF!
There a WOOF!
Everywhere a WOOF! WOOF!
Old MacDonald had a farm,
E-I-E-I-O!

69

I Had a Rooster

I had a rooster, and my rooster pleased me.
I fed my rooster by the green apple tree.
My little rooster went cock-a-doodle-doo.
Dee doodle-ee doodle-ee doodle-ee do.

I had a cat, and my cat pleased me.
I fed my cat by the green apple tree.
My little kitty went miaow, miaow, miaow, miaow.
My little rooster went cock-a-doodle-doo.
Dee doodle-ee doodle-ee doodle-ee do.

I had a cow, and my cow pleased me.
I fed my cow by the green apple tree.
My big, old cow went moo, moo, moo, moo.
My little kitty went miaow, miaow, miaow, miaow.
My little rooster went cock-a-doodle-doo.
Dee doodle-ee doodle-ee doodle-ee do.

Goosey, Goosey, Gander

Goosey, goosey, gander,
Whither shall I wander?
Upstairs and downstairs,
And in my lady's chamber.
There I met an old man,
Who wouldn't say his prayers.
So I took him by the left leg,
And threw him down the stairs.

The Farmer in the Dell

The farmer in the dell, the farmer in the dell,
Hi-ho, the derry-o, the farmer in the dell.

The farmer takes a wife, the farmer takes a wife,
Hi-ho, the derry-o, the farmer takes a wife.

The wife takes a child, the wife takes a child,
Hi-ho, the derry-o, the wife takes a child.

The child takes a dog, the child takes a dog,
Hi-ho, the derry-o, the child takes a dog.

The dog takes a cat, the dog takes a cat,
Hi-ho, the derry-o, the dog takes a cat.

The cat takes a mouse, the cat takes a mouse,
Hi-ho, the derry-o, the cat takes a mouse.

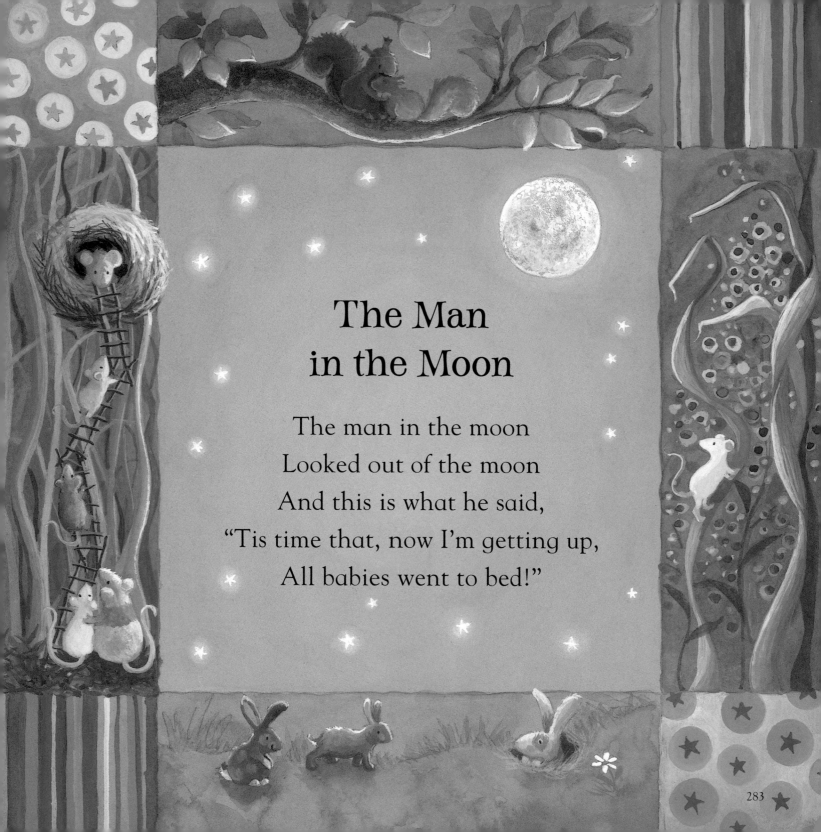

The Man
in the Moon

The man in the moon
Looked out of the moon
And this is what he said,
"Tis time that, now I'm getting up,
All babies went to bed!"

Twinkle, Twinkle, Little Star

Twinkle, twinkle, little star,
How I wonder what you are.
Up above the world so high,
Like a diamond in the sky!
Twinkle, twinkle, little star,
How I wonder what you are.

The animals are all in bed.
    I curl up snugly too.
My night-light's gentle, golden glow
    Stays with us all night through.

Lighthouse, with your golden beams,
    Wish us all, "Goodnight, sweet dreams!"

When turtles hatch out from their eggs,
   A beacon lights the ground!
Flip-flap! They hurry to the sea
   And swim off safe and sound.

Lighthouse, cast your gleaming ray –
   Help the turtles find their way.

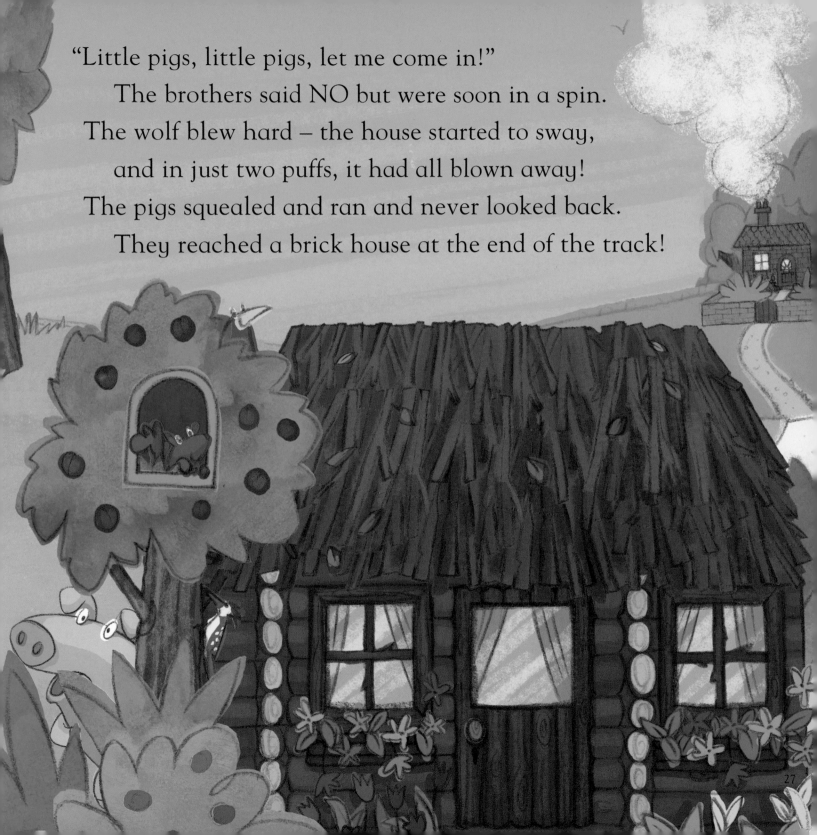

"Little pigs, little pigs, let me come in!"
The brothers said NO but were soon in a spin.
The wolf blew hard – the house started to sway,
and in just two puffs, it had all blown away!
The pigs squealed and ran and never looked back.
They reached a brick house at the end of the track!

27

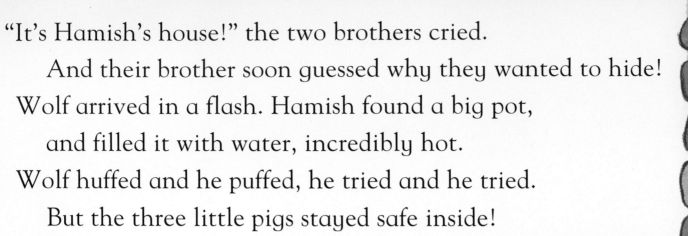

"It's Hamish's house!" the two brothers cried.
    And their brother soon guessed why they wanted to hide!
Wolf arrived in a flash. Hamish found a big pot,
    and filled it with water, incredibly hot.
Wolf huffed and he puffed, he tried and he tried.
    But the three little pigs stayed safe inside!

So Wolf climbed on the roof and stamped on one spot,
then slid down the chimney and into the pot!
Then out of the door, the pigs watched him go –
his bottom was burning, and hurting him so!
"Hip, hip hooray!" the pigs sang together.
"We'll stay in this house for ever and ever!"

How Many Miles to Babylon?

How many miles to Babylon?
Three score miles and ten.
Can I get there by candlelight?
Yes, and back again.
If your heels are nimble and light,
You may get there by candlelight.

5 Minute
Nursery
Rhymes

LITTLE TIGER PRESS
London

Humpty Dumpty's Favourite Counting Rhymes 13

LITTLE JACK HORNER'S FAVOURITE FOOD RHYMES 153

Mary Mary's Favourite Garden Rhymes

LITTLE BOY BLUE'S FAVOURITE CHILDHOOD RHYMES 215

Humpty Dumpty's Favourite Counting Rhymes

One, Two, Buckle My Shoe

One, two,
Buckle my shoe,

Three, four,
Knock at the door,

Five, six,
Pick up sticks,

Seven, eight,
Lay them straight,

Nine, ten,
A big, fat hen.

14

There Was an Old Woman

There was an old woman
Who lived in a shoe.
She had so many children,
She didn't know what to do.

Rub-a-dub-dub

Rub-a-dub-dub,
Three men in a tub,
And who do you think they be?
The butcher, the baker,
The candlestick maker,
Turn 'em out, knaves all three!

One, Two, Three, Four, Five

One, two, three, four, five,
Once I caught a fish alive.
Six, seven, eight, nine, ten,
Then I let it go again.

Humpty Dumpty

Humpty Dumpty sat on a wall,
Humpty Dumpty had a great fall.
All the King's horses
and all the King's men,
Couldn't put Humpty
Together again.

She'll Be Coming
Round the Mountain

She'll be coming round the mountain when she comes.
She'll be coming round the mountain when she comes.
She'll be coming round the mountain,
She'll be coming round the mountain,
She'll be coming round the mountain when she comes.

She'll be driving six white horses when she comes.
She'll be driving six white horses when she comes.
She'll be driving six white horses,
She'll be driving six white horses,
She'll be driving six white horses when she comes.

Hickory, Dickory, Dock

Hickory, dickory, dock,
The mouse ran up the clock.
The clock struck one,
The mouse ran down.
Hickory, dickory, dock.

The Three Little Pigs

Once upon a time in a fairytale wood
lived three little pigs who were simple and good.
There was no room at home – the pigs had all grown,
each wanted to build a new place of their own.
"Watch out for the wolf!" said their mum to all three.
"He's big, bad and hungry – he'd have you for tea!"

Her eldest son, Hamish, said, "Mother, don't worry,
    Wolf's on a holiday – no need to hurry.
There's time to build houses, safe, strong and sound,
    deep in the woods where they'll never be found!"
Now Hamish was clever, but his brothers were not,
    and their mother's advice they quickly forgot . . .

The youngest pig, Hampton, thought he was right
to build his new home from what first caught his sight!
"A house made of straw! Now that will be best!
I'll build it so quickly, I can soon have a rest!"
But when winter came, it was lonely and cold,
and the wolf soon showed up – hungry and bold.

He called through the window with an evil grin,
   "Little pig, little pig, let me come in!"
Hampton squealed, "No, by the hairs on my chin!"
   "Then I'll huff and I'll puff and I'll blow your house in!"
In one puff, the flimsy house was no more.
   Poor Hampton stood shaking, surrounded by straw!

Now Hampton thought he could escape this fix
by running to Hamilton's house of sticks!
But a house made of sticks (though quite quick to make)
was draughty and flimsy and such a mistake.
So the two brothers were not safe for long.
Yes, you've guessed that Wolfie soon came along!

With a BAAA! BAAA! here,
And a BAAA! BAAA! there . . .

Baaa!

Baaa!

51

. . . Here a *BAAA!*
There a *BAAA!*
Everywhere a *BAAA! BAAA!*
Old MacDonald had a farm,
E-I-E-I-O!

Baaa!

Baaa!

Old MacDonald had a farm,
E-I-E-I-O!
And on that farm
he had some cows,
E-I-E-I-O!
With a MOO! MOO! here,
And a MOO! MOO! there . . .

Moo!

Moo!

Moo!
Moo!

. . . Here a MOO!
There a MOO!
Everywhere a MOO! MOO!
Old MacDonald had a farm,
E-I-E-I-O!

Old MacDonald had a farm,
E-I-E-I-O!
And on that farm he had some pigs,
E-I-E-I-O!
With an OINK! OINK! here,
And an OINK! OINK! there . . .

. . . Here an OINK!
There an OINK!
Everywhere an OINK! OINK!
Old MacDonald had a farm,
E-I-E-I-O!

5 MINUTE NURSERY RHYMES

LITTLE TIGER PRESS
1 The Coda Centre
189 Munster Road
London SW6 6AW
www.littletigerpress.com

First published in Great Britain 2013

This volume copyright © Little Tiger Press 2013
Cover artwork copyright © Gill Guile 2012

The acknowledgements on page 286-287 constitute an
extension of this copyright page

All rights reserved

ISBN 978-1-84895-636-0

Printed in China
LTP/1800/0524/1112
2 4 6 8 10 9 7 5 3 1

'Here We Go Round the Mulberry Bush' illustrations copyright © Gill Guile 2012; 'I Had a Little Nut Tree' illustrated by Sanja Rešček, copyright © Little Tiger Press 2006; 'Mary Mary, Quite Contrary', illustrations copyright © Gill Guile 2013; 'Lavender's Blue' illustrations copyright © Gail Yerrill 2008; 'Roses are Red' illustrations copyright © Cee Biscoe 2012; *One Magical Morning* copyright © Claire Freedman 2005, illustrations copyright © Louise Ho 2005; 'It's Raining, It's Pouring' illustrations copyright © Gill Guile 2013; 'Rain, Rain, Go Away' illustrations copyright © Cee Biscoe 2012; 'The Green Grass Grew All Around' illustrations copyright © Corinne Bittler 2009; 'Early to Bed' illustrations copyright © Gavin Scott 2010; 'Red Sky at Night' illustrated by Sanja Rešček, copyright © Little Tiger Press 2006; 'Brahms' Lullaby' illustrations copyright © Gail Yerrill 2008; 'I See the Moon' illustrations copyright © Gill Guile 2012.

'Monday's Child' illustrated by Rachel Baines, copyright © Little Tiger Press 2010; 'Diddle Diddle Dumpling' illustrated by Sanja Rešček, copyright © Little Tiger Press 2006; 'There Was a Little Girl' illustrations copyright © Gaby Hansen 2005; 'Are You Sleeping?' illustrated by Sanja Rešček, copyright © Little Tiger Press 2006; 'Lucy Locket' illustrations copyright © Gill Guile 2013; 'Little Boy Blue' illustrated by Sanja Rešček, copyright © Little Tiger Press 2006; 'Lazy Mary' illustrations copyright © Sanja Rešček 2009; *Goldilocks and the Three Bears* copyright © Caterpillar Books Ltd 2012, illustrations copyright © Jenny Arthur 2012; 'Girls and Boys, Come Out to Play' illustrated by Sanja Rešček, copyright © Little Tiger Press 2006; 'Bonnie Girls and Bonnie Boys' copyright © Little Tiger Press 2008, illustrations copyright © Gail Yerrill 2008; 'Matthew, Mark, Luke and John' illustrated by Sanja Rešček, copyright © Little Tiger Press 2006; *You're My Little Star* copyright © Julia Hubery 2012, illustrations copyright © Cee Biscoe 2012.

Every effort has been made to trace copyright holders, but if there are any omissions the publishers apologise for any copyright transgression and would like to hear from any copyright holders not acknowledged.

'Rock-a-bye, Baby' illustrated by Sanja Rešček, copyright © Little Tiger Press 2006; 'Star Light, Star Bright' illustrations copyright © Gail Yerrill 2008; 'Wee Willie Winkie' illustrations copyright © Gill Guile 2012; 'Aiken Drum' illustrated by Sanja Rešček, copyright © Little Tiger Press 2006; 'Day is Done' illustrations copyright © Gail Yerrill 2008; 'Now the Day is Over' illustrated by Sanja Rešček, copyright © Little Tiger Press 2006; 'My Little Baby' copyright © Little Tiger Press 2008, illustrations copyright © Gail Yerrill 2008; *A Kiss Goodnight* copyright © Claire Freedman 2007, illustrations copyright © Alison Edgson, Stephen Gulbis, Sophy Williams 2007; 'Golden Slumbers' illustrations copyright © Gill Guile 2012; 'Hush-a-bye, Baby' copyright © Little Tiger Press 2008, illustrations copyright © Gail Yerrill 2008; 'God Bless the Moon' illustrations copyright © Gail Yerrill 2008; 'When The Sun Goes Down to Bed' copyright © Little Tiger Press 2008, illustrated by Sanja Rešček, copyright © Little Tiger Press 2006; 'All Through the Night' illustrations copyright © Gail Yerrill 2008; *My Little Night-light* copyright © Claire Freedman 2008, illustrations copyright © Alison Edgson 2008; 'Twinkle, Twinkle, Little Star' illustrations copyright © Gill Guile 2012; 'The Man in the Moon' illustrations copyright © Gail Yerrill 2008.

Additional artwork by Gill Guile and Sanja Rešček.

Acknowledgements

'One, Two, Buckle My Shoe' illustrated by Sanja Rešček, copyright © Little Tiger Press 2006; 'There Was an Old Woman' illustrations copyright © Gill Guile 2013; 'Rub-a-dub-dub' illustrated by Sanja Rešček, copyright © Little Tiger Press 2006; 'One, Two, Three, Four, Five' illustrations copyright © Gill Guile 2012; 'Humpty Dumpty' illustrated by Sanja Rešček, copyright © Little Tiger Press 2006; 'She'll Be Coming Round the Mountain' illustrations copyright © Gill Guile 2012; 'Hickory, Dickory, Dock' illustrated by Sanja Rešček, copyright © Little Tiger Press 2006; *The Three Little Pigs* copyright © Caterpillar Books Ltd 2009, illustrations copyright © Jenny Arthur 2009; 'How Many Miles to Babylon?' illustrations copyright © Gail Yerrill 2008; 'The Grand Old Duke of York' illustrations copyright © Gill Guile 2013; 'Five Green and Speckled Frogs' illustrations copyright © Maria Maddocks 2013; 'Three Blind Mice' illustrated by Sanja Rešček, copyright © Little Tiger Press 2006; 'Here is the Beehive' illustrations copyright © Jo Moon 2009; 'Over in the Meadow' illustrations copyright © Julie Fletcher 2009; 'One, Two, Stars on High' copyright © Little Tiger Press 2008, illustrated by Alison Edgson, illustrations copyright © Little Tiger Press 2011; 'Five in the Bed' illustrated by Rachel Baines, copyright © Little Tiger Press 2010.

'Baa, Baa, Black Sheep' illustrations copyright © Gill Guile 2012; 'Mary Had a Little Lamb' illustrated by Sanja Rešček, copyright © Little Tiger Press 2006; 'Little Bo-Peep' illustrated by Sanja Rešček, copyright © Little Tiger Press 2006; 'Six Little Ducks' illustrations copyright © Caroline Pedler 2008; 'Cock-a-doodle-doo!' illustrations copyright © Gill Guile 2012; *Old MacDonald Had a Farm* illustrations copyright © Daniel Howarth 2011; 'I Had a Rooster' illustrated by Veronica Vasylenko, copyright © Little Tiger Press 2011; 'Goosey, Goosey, Gander' illustrated by Sanja Rešček, copyright © Little Tiger Press 2006; 'The Farmer in the Dell' illustrations copyright © Anna Lewis 2012; 'Hickety Pickety, My Black Hen' illustrations copyright © Julie Fletcher 2007, Anna Lubecka 2009; 'Sleep, Baby, Sleep' illustrations copyright © Gill Guile 2012.

'Jack Be Nimble' illustrations copyright © Gill Guile 2012; 'Ring-a-ring o' Roses' illustrated by Sanja Rešček, copyright © Little Tiger Press 2006; 'B-I-N-G-O' illustrations copyright © Maria Maddocks 2013; 'Row, Row, Row Your Boat' illustrations copyright © Gill Guile 2012;

The Wheels on the Bus illustrations copyright © Polona Lovsin 2011; 'Skip to My Lou' illustrations copyright © Gail Yerrill 2011; 'Jack and Jill' illustrations copyright © Gill Guile 2012; 'London Bridge' illustrated by Louise Ho, copyright © Little Tiger Press 2007; 'If You're Happy and You Know It' illustrations copyright © Jenny Arthur 2011; 'See-saw, Margery Daw' illustrated by Sanja Rešček, copyright © Little Tiger Press 2006; 'Head, Shoulders, Knees and Toes' illustrations copyright © Gaby Hansen 2005; 'Teddy Bear, Teddy Bear' illustrated by Sanja Rešček, copyright © Little Tiger Press 2006.

'Little Miss Muffet' illustrated by Sanja Rešček, copyright © Little Tiger Press 2006; 'Ladybird, Ladybird' illustrations copyright © Kimberley Scott 2011; 'Incy Wincy Spider' illustrated by Sanja Rešček, copyright © Little Tiger Press 2006; *Incy Wincy Goes Flying*, previously published as *Incy Wincy Spider*, copyright © Keith Chapman 2005, illustrations copyright © Jack Tickle 2005; 'Pussy Cat, Pussy Cat' illustrations copyright Gill Guile 2013; 'The Owl and the Pussy Cat' illustrations copyright © Gail Yerrill 2008; 'Come to the Window' illustrations copyright © Gail Yerrill 2008; 'Where Has My Little Dog Gone?' illustrations copyright © Sharon Harmer 2012; 'All The Pretty Little Horses' illustrations copyright © Gail Yerrill 2008; 'Hush, Little Baby' illustrated by Sanja Rešček, copyright © Little Tiger Press 2006.

'Pat-a-cake' illustrations copyright © Gill Guile 2013; 'Hot Cross Buns' illustrations copyright © Tomislav Zlatic 2009; 'This Little Piggy' illustrations copyright © Gill Guile 2013; 'Peter, Peter, Pumpkin Eater' illustrated by Sanja Rešček, copyright © Little Tiger Press 2006; 'Little Jack Horner' illustrations copyright © Gill Guile 2012; 'Old King Cole' illustrations copyright © Gill Guile 2012; 'Sing a Song of Sixpence' illustrated by Sanja Rešček, copyright © Little Tiger Press 2006; 'Pease Porridge Hot' illustrated by Sanja Rešček, copyright © Little Tiger Press 2006; 'The Princess and the Pea' copyright © Little Tiger Press 2011, illustrations copyright © Rachel Baines 2011; 'Sippity Sup' illustrations copyright © Gaby Hansen 2005; 'The Muffin Man' illustrated by Sanja Rešček, copyright © Little Tiger Press 2006; 'Oats, Peas, Beans and Barley' illustrated by Louise Ho, copyright © Little Tiger Press 2007; 'To Market, To Market' illustrations copyright © Tomislav Zlatic 2009; 'Hey Diddle Diddle' illustrations copyright © Gill Guile 2012.